D0551401

# 101 SALIVATIONS

## FOR THE LOVE OF DOGS

EBURY
PRESS

# 101 SALIVATIONS

## FOR THE LOVE OF DOGS

RACHAEL HALE

FOR ALL THE DOGS WE HAVE LOVED
AND LOST.
FOR THE DOGS WE STILL LOVE
AND FOR ALL THE DOGS WE WILL LOVE
IN THE FUTURE.

On a brisk walk through the park one morning, I found Darcy, a tiny, trembling angel on my feet. We were friends from the start, but it was a bond born from fear rather than friendship.

A few minutes before, Darcy, a jaunty little Dachshund, had been trotting nonchalantly along the path in a leafy inner-city park. That was until she spied us approaching — me flanked by two strapping Newfoundlands named Henry and George.

When Darcy clapped eyes on these two hulking beasts ambling towards her, she mustered all the speed she had in her miniature legs and sought refuge. But rather than turn on her heels, she ran straight for us. In a flash, she had scooted between my legs and planted herself on top of my feet, burying her claws into the flesh for further solace. An inch or so taller and a pinch bolder, Darcy could finally eyeball the big dogs, by now bewildered by the little one's dash to safety atop my toes.

It was chance meetings like this one in the park, or on windswept beaches and street corners, that helped me fill the pages of this book with the incredibly diverse range of personalities, shapes and sizes you encounter in the dog world. In my quest to find 101 special dogs, I often approached dog owners meandering through the parks that I visited every day with my dog, Henry Miller. When I asked if I could capture their dogs on film, every one of them replied, "Yes, yes, we'd love you to."

Perhaps their enthusiasm stemmed from the pride and sheer joy they get from their dogs; maybe they wanted to share the love they hold for their animals with us, in the hope that you may see your own cherished hound reflected in their images.

My earliest memories of photography are taking snaps of the family pets. Looking back it was perhaps inevitable that I would end up in this wonderful profession. My paternal grandparents were both keen amateur photographers who travelled the world shooting beautiful images.

I still have the "Box Brownies" they owned, and even today I use my grandmother's twin-lens reflex Rolleiflex camera, now more than 70 years old. It's been driven over and dropped down stairs, yet it still takes exquisite shots.

I shot most of the images for this book using a 4 x 5 inch large-format camera, like the old-fashioned box with the black cape over the back. I love the images it creates – you can almost reach into the picture and feel the animal's fur. The shallow depth of field is incredible; it draws you to the dog, especially its eyes. Yet, using the large-format camera is probably the most difficult way to capture animals on film. If the dog moves, which they are inclined to do often and without warning, you have to take the film out and refocus. It's a true game of patience, not point and shoot. But it's what I'm used to working with, and what I really enjoy.

Some dogs go beyond the call of duty to please the lens. Take, for example, Bruno the Italian Spinone. Bruno was 18 months old and everything you could ask for in a man – young, active and very intelligent.

When we asked him to champ down on a cigar we expected him to spit it out just as fast. At first he did just that, unimpressed with the taste of a cigar – which, I can assure you, was unlit. With gaffer tape wound around one end, Bruno readily accepted the cheroot between his teeth. With his paws crossed, Bruno looked like a genuine Mafioso – all that was missing was a gold chain! It would not have worked with just any dog; you have to find one with the right attitude.

I am always mindful that you cannot force an animal to do anything they do not want to … you can lead a dog to the lens, but you cannot make him grin. Even when the owners are begging their dogs to perform for the camera, I would never put an animal through any stress to obtain a certain look. But there are ways to hurdle tricky situations, if you keep your wits about you. I am sure I have earned a degree in animal psychology from this experience!

I don't believe in the old cliché: don't work with animals or children. I have worked with both, and I've adored them equally. I love dogs, especially, for their innocence and their unconditional love. It's hard to imagine life without the joy and companionship they bring. I consider myself one of the luckiest people on earth to be able to combine my two passions – animals and photography. And I would be happy if I could do this for the rest of my life, with my beloved Henry at my side.     RACHAEL HALE

In a dog-eat-dog world,

it is the dogmatic domain

of dog lovers

to offer dogdom a dog's chance

to rise above the dog days

for a doggone good time.

AMERICAN KENNEL CLUB GAZETTE

AMBER
1. VIZSLA ▶

3. ENGLISH BULLDOG BRIT DOG ▶

5. MACTAVISH GORDON SETTER ▶

6. JIMMY BRUSSELS GRIFFON ▼

7. HUNTER GREAT DANE ▲

# MUD PUPPY

8. MAREMMA SHEEPDOG ▶

# GEORGE & HUGO

◀ 9. NEWFOUNDLAND

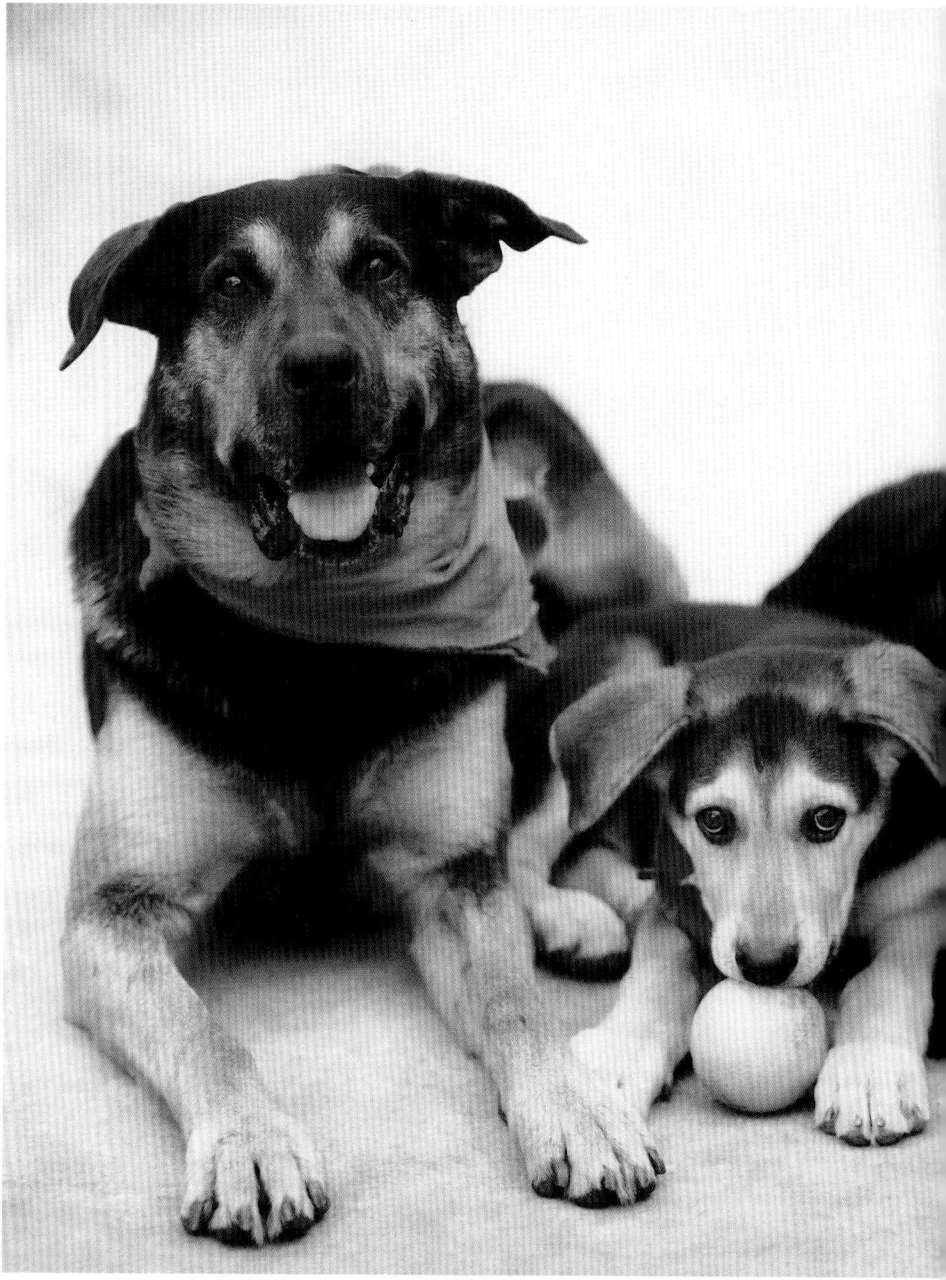

10. HERCULES, DOC, PAINTBRUSH & CHOOKEE HUNTAWAY CROSS ▼

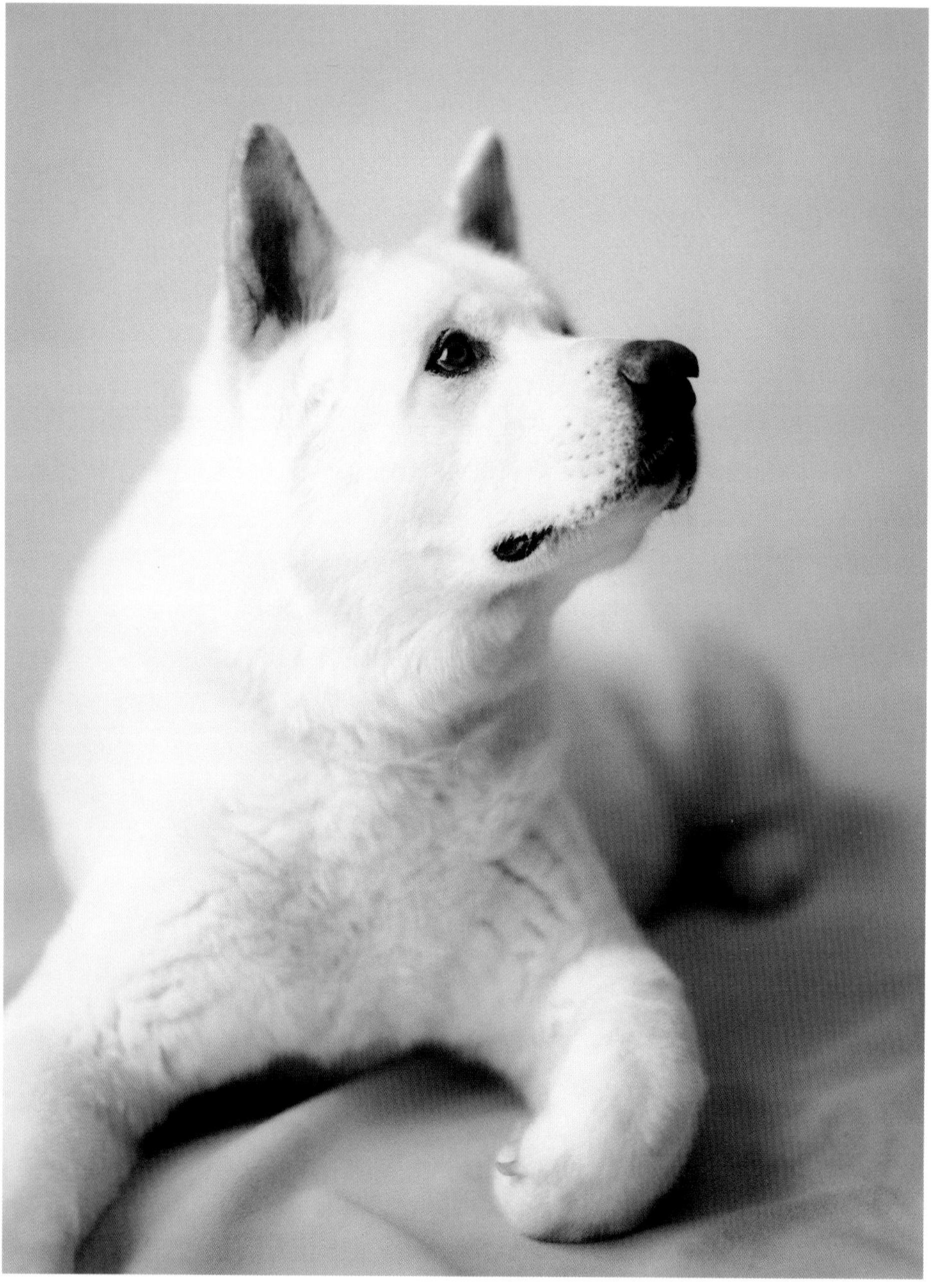

11. HIRO AKITA ◀

12. AMIGO BLUE HEELER ▶

A dog has one aim in life...

to bestow his heart.

J R ACKERLEY

MUFFIN
13. BORDER COLLIE CROSS ▶

No one appreciates

the very special genius

of your conversation

as the dog does.

**CHRISTOPHER MORLEY**

18. BELLA CURLY-COATED RETRIEVER ▶

20. HOTAI BOSTON TERRIER ▲

21. PYRENEAN SHEPHERD ▶

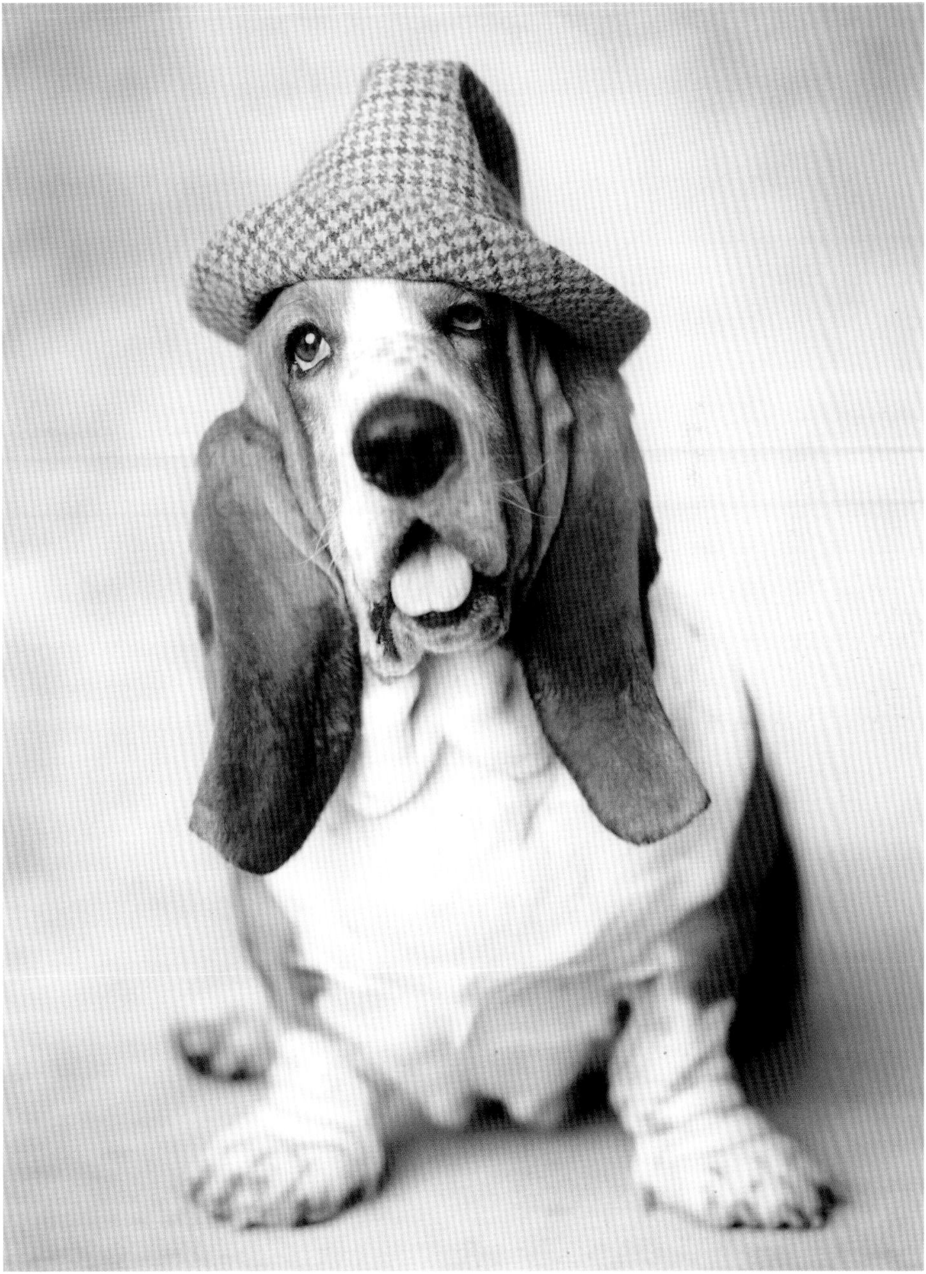

22. SAM BASSET HOUND ▲▼

The average dog is a nicer person

than the average person.

**ANDREW A ROONEY**

27. KHAN & LUCKY KANGAL DOG ▶

OLLY & MADDY
29. IRISH SETTER ▶

▲ 31. BEN & BELLA **BLOODHOUND**

I don't think he has any idea

he's a dog, not really.

Of course, he thinks he has

a rather odd figure for a man.

DODIE SMITH

33. CHEEKO PUG ▲

▲ 35. DOMINIC AMERICAN COCKER SPANIEL

37. RAMONE STAFFORDSHIRE BULL TERRIER CROSS ▶

Happiness is a warm puppy.

**CHARLES M SCHULZ**

40. MONTY DALMATIAN ▶

# BRUCE

◀ 41. WEIMARANER

A dog is a dog except when he is facing you.

Then he is Mr. Dog. HAITIAN PROVERB

42. CONAN THE BARBARIAN RHODESIAN RIDGEBACK CROSS ▲▼

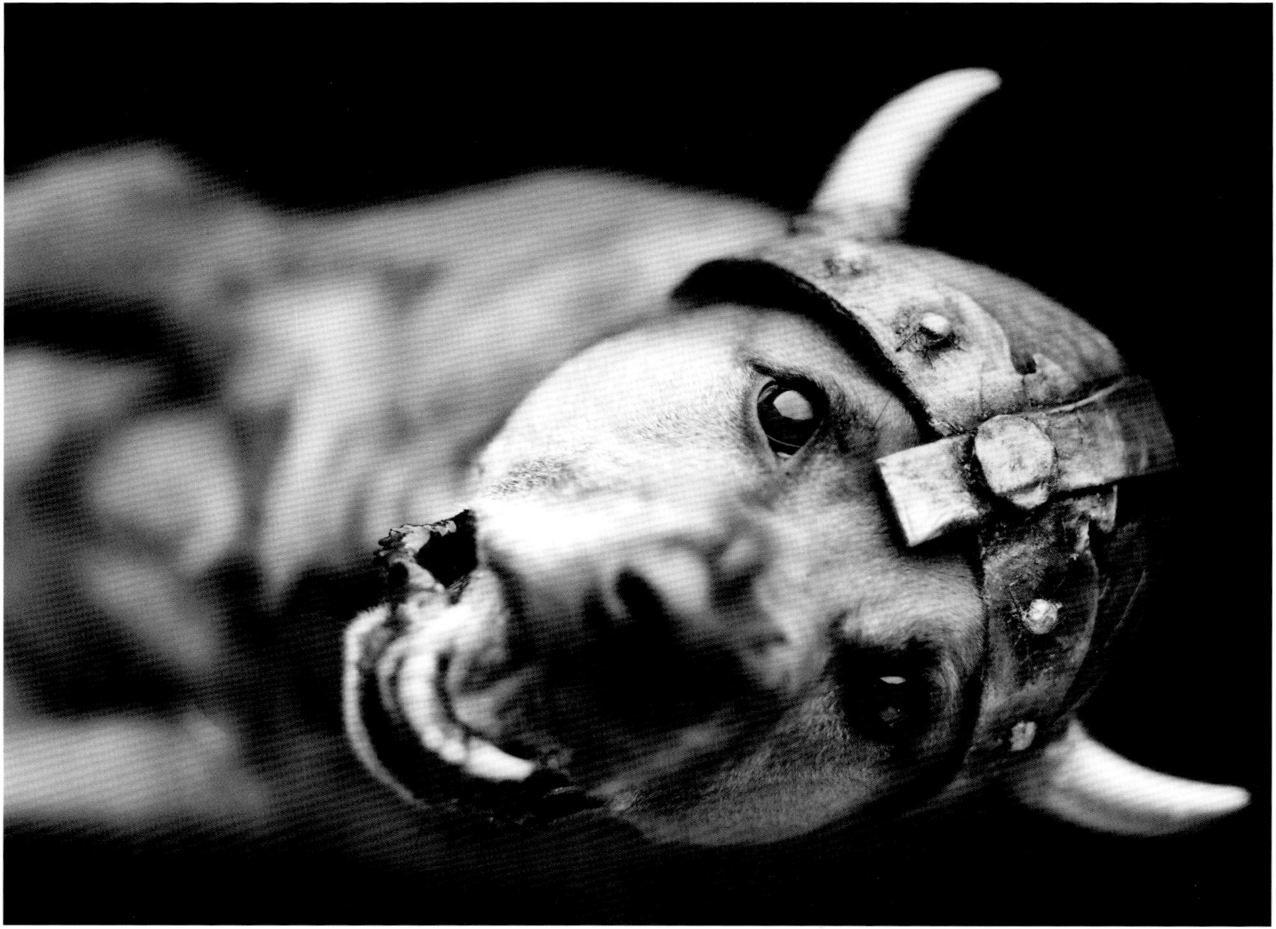

# NEO

43. NEAPOLITAN MASTIFF ▶

▲ 44. BLITZEN & DONNER GERMAN SHORT-HAIRED POINTER

ZENITH

45. BOXER CROSS ▶

46. ILLBRUCK & SABRINA BULLMASTIFF ▼

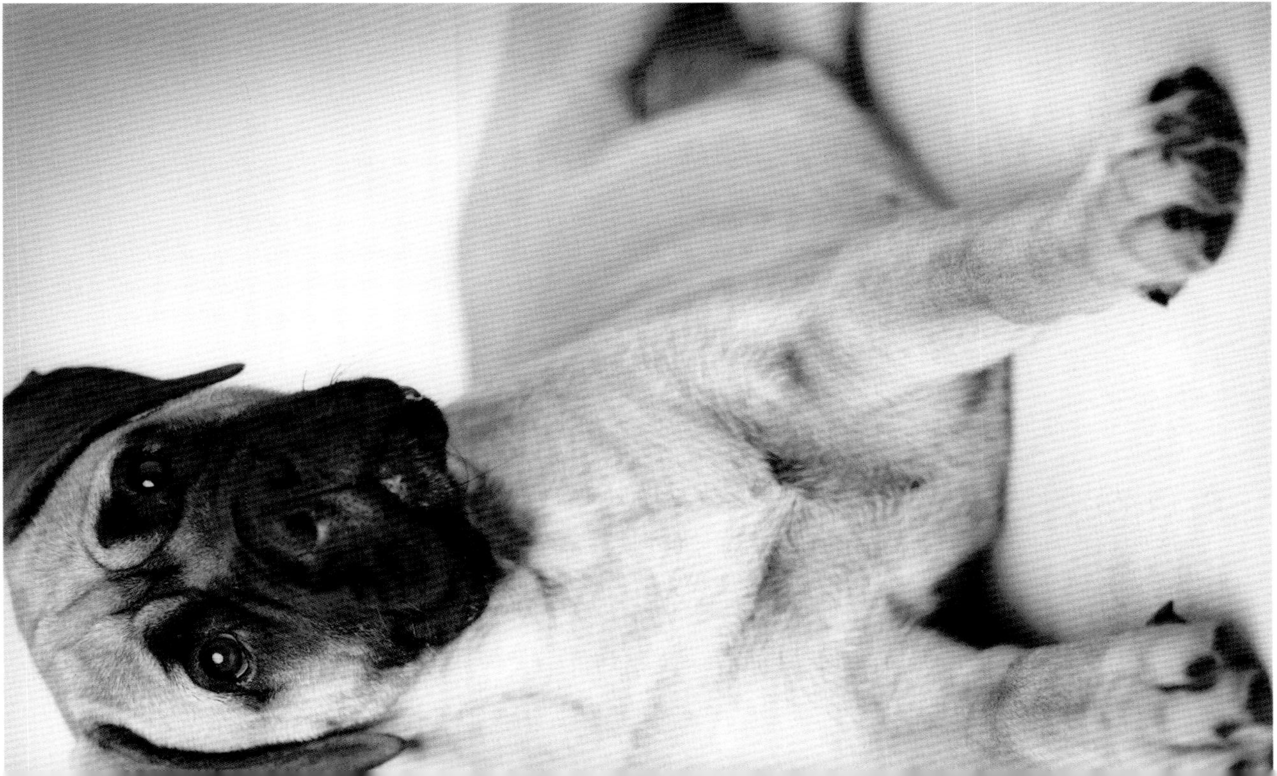

You can run with

the big dogs...

...or sit on the porch and bark.

**WALLACE ARNOLD**

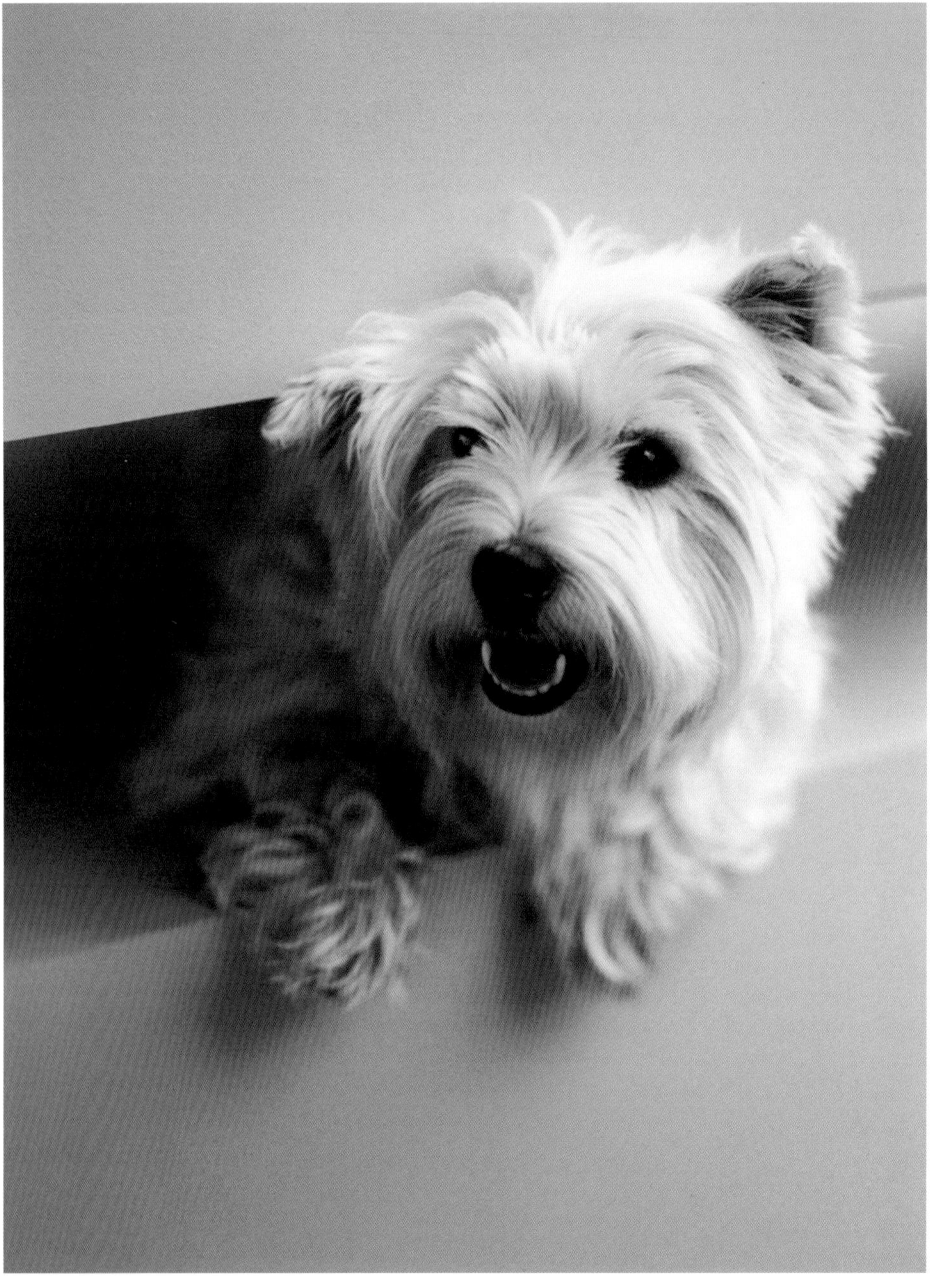

49. RALPH WEST HIGHLAND WHITE TERRIER ▼

MY OH MY

53. LEXI LÖWCHEN ▲

If you are a dog

and your owner suggests

that you wear a sweater...

suggest that he wear a tail.

**FRAN LEBOWITZ**

▲ 56. LENNY PULI

# RIOT & BRIAR

◀ 57. STANDARD POODLE

What feeling do we ever find

To equal among human kind

A dog's fidelity!

**THOMAS HARDY**

◄ 61. CLEOPATRA PUG

# KEESHA

62. KEESHOND ▶

# FURBY

◀ 63. POMERANIAN

▲ 65. TALI BASENJI

# HENRY

66. NEWFOUNDLAND ▶

▲ HENRY & PIPI

68. TIGER LILLIE CHINESE CRESTED ▶

BAILLIE

◀ 69. BEARDED COLLIE

It is fatal to let any dog know

that he is funny, for he immediately loses his

head and starts hamming it up.

**P G WODEHOUSE**

70. PIPPA AUSTRALIAN SHEPHERD ▶

# WINGS & RANA

◀ 71. IRISH WOLFHOUND

73. OSCAR KERRY BLUE TERRIER ▶

74. FRANCIS OF LOCHRANZO ENGLISH SPRINGER SPANIEL ▶

# BRUNO

◀ 75. SPINONE ITALIANO

76. WOOKIE, MARTHA, OAKE, MIMMI & SKYE LEONBERGER ▶

78/79. NANCY & GRIFF BORDER TERRIER AND BEARDED COLLIE CROSS ▲

A dog has the soul of a philosopher. **PLATO**

80. SAM ENGLISH SETTER ▶

# GYPSY

◀ 81. BULL TERRIER

# RIPLEY

84. CHINESE SHAR-PEI ▶

JACK

◀ 85. SPOODLE

DOUGAL
86. LABRADOODLE ▶

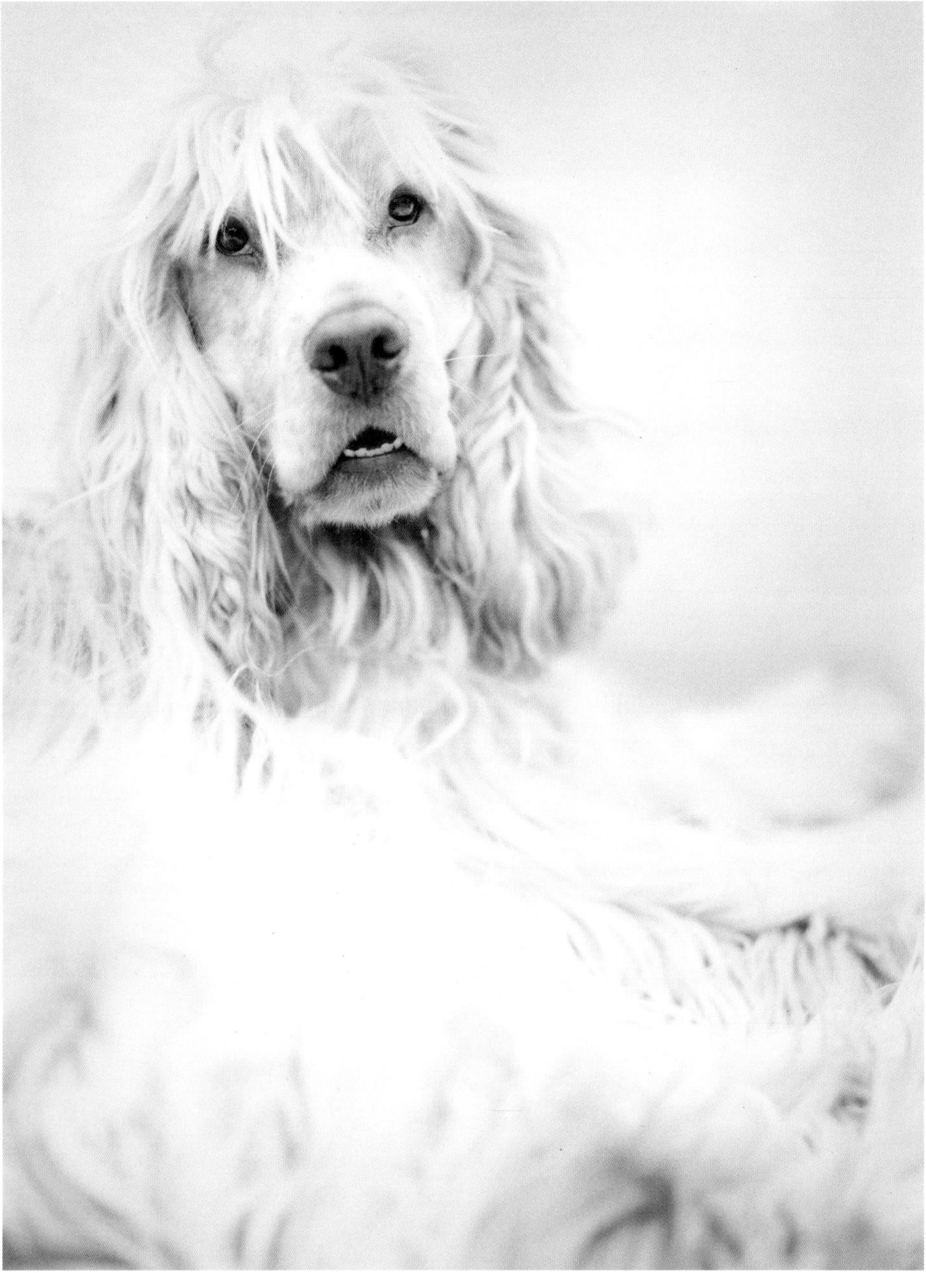

87. BANJO ENGLISH COCKER SPANIEL ▼

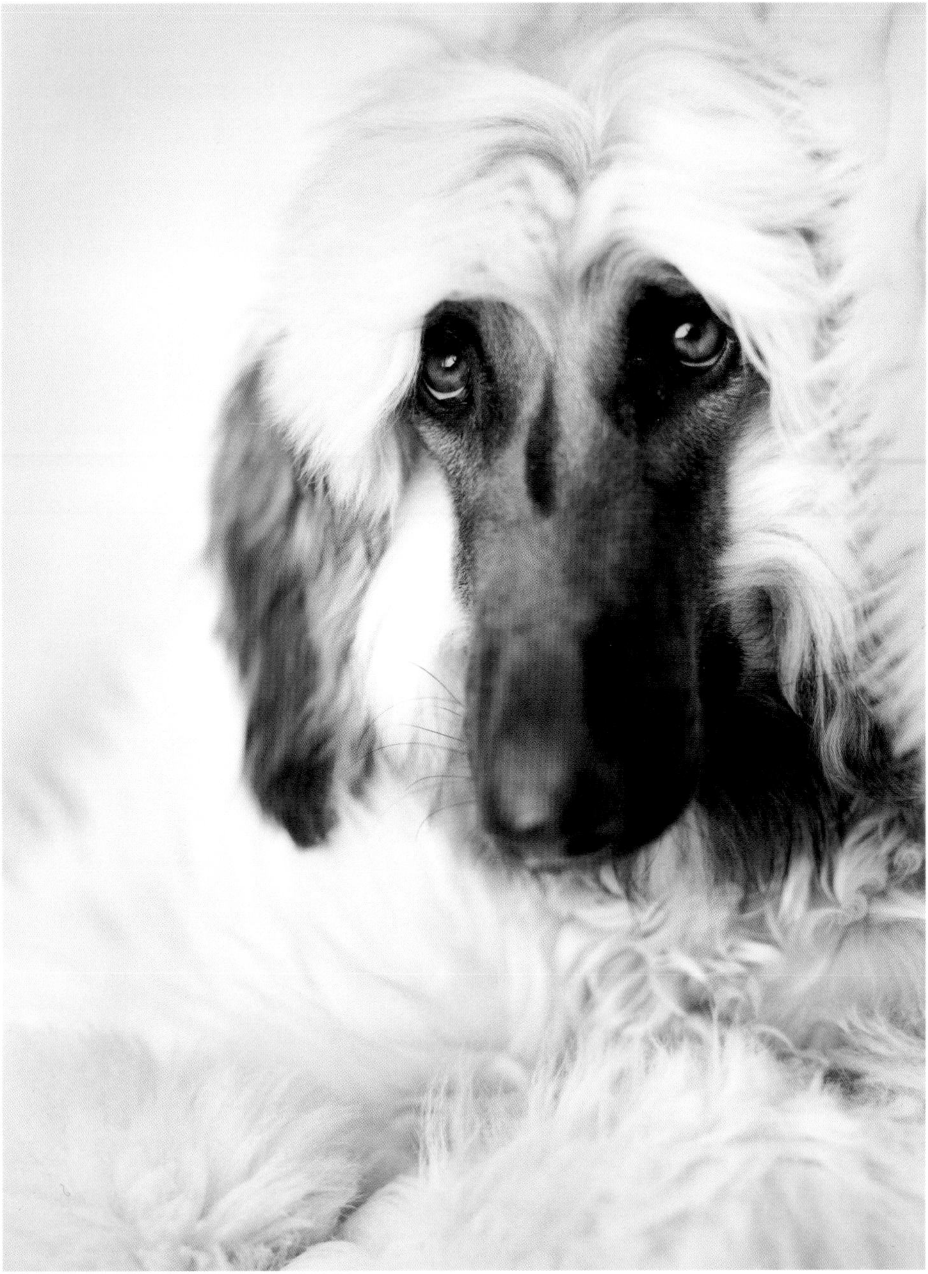

88. YASMINE AFGHAN HOUND ▼

89/90. MOCHA & CINO AUSTRALIAN KELPIE AND SIBERIAN HUSKY ▲ ▶

# TUI & COCO

91. ROUGH COLLIE ▶

The dog

is the god of frolic.

**WALT WHITMAN**

◀ 92. ELVIS BERNESE MOUNTAIN DOG

MISS ELLIE

**93. TIBETAN SPANIEL** ▶

# JUDY

**96. IRISH WATER SPANIEL** ▶

My little dog —

a heartbeat at my feet.

EDITH WHARTON

▲ 97. DARCY DACHSHUND

99. IAGO JACK RUSSELL TERRIER ▶

# 100 + 1

100/101. HAMISH & FLYNN CHIHUAHUA AND GREAT DANE ▶

# INDEX

## 14.
### JAPANESE SPITZ
Blackie – six months old

Blackie wasn't the dog I had come to photograph. Standing at the door was the Japanese Spitz I was supposed to work with – wearing a bright green cast on his broken leg. Blackie, meanwhile, was in the backyard rolling in mud, but after a bath in the kitchen sink, proved to be the perfect model.

## 15.
### SAMOYED
Sasha – seven years old

The first shot was the best shot of Sasha, a Samoyed with a smile permanently painted on her face.

## 16.
### DOBERMAN PINSCHER
Dobie – four years old

Dobie was one of the most gentle and affectionate dogs I've worked with. He kept the rose in his mouth for just a moment – the gentleman in him would rather have left it at my feet.

## 17.
### SALUKI
Abigail – four years old

Abigail was one of my very first photographic models and she was as professional as she was beautiful with her crown of roses.

## 18.
### CURLY-COATED RETRIEVER
Bella – 11 years old

Bella's verve and grace, as she dashed into the sea time and time again to retrieve the tennis ball, belied her 11 years. She would stare at the ball, held just above the camera before it disappeared into the surf, oblivious to the fact she was being photographed.

## 19.
### AFFENPINSCHER
Monkey – one and a half years old

Not every blinding flash of brilliance works. I had a special handbag crafted for Monkey, who is toted around town over his owner's shoulder. But when the first photo didn't look right – Monkey got lost in his accessory – a simpler pose did the trick.

## 20.
### BOSTON TERRIER
Hotai – two months old

Hotai was one of nine puppies, but his charming face promoted him from the pack. The cacophony from his envious brothers and sisters made it a real challenge to keep Hotai's attention.

## 21.
### PYRENEAN SHEPHERD
Max – three years old

Without complaint, being the true champion that he is, Max had no trouble balancing on little mountains of stones, even though it would be a major feat for any dog. There's a reason why the Pyrenean is called the Gentleman of the Mountain.

## 22.
### BASSET HOUND
Sam – six years old

My grandfather lived in this old houndstooth hat, but it fitted Sam perfectly, as if it had been made for hound rather than human.

## 23.
### SAINT BERNARD
Sharky and Annie – four months old

We had to lift these brother and sister puppies on to the chair and they were dead weights in our arms. Then it was a hefty challenge trying to squash them in to fit!

## 24.
### BOXER
Cassius – eight years old

Cassius has had a tough life, living in numerous homes before being adopted by friends of mine at the age of six. The look on his face says he is now a happy, well-adjusted dog.

## 25.
### STAFFORDSHIRE BULL TERRIER CROSS
Loki – nine years old

This gentle-natured dog, owned by animal trainer Marie Manderson, adores kittens, and has been mother to many. He was totally at ease with Gingernut asleep on his head.

## 26.
### PAPILLON
Cory – ten years old

If it wasn't for a chance visit to the bathroom, I would never have been bowled over by Cory. While photographing Max, the Pyrenean Shepherd, I opened the bathroom door and 15 little Papillons spilled out. While the others ran around madly, Cory stood his ground, guarding his dog biscuit.

## 27.
## KANGAL DOG
Khan – one year old

Kangal Dogs protect sheep from predators. When I arrived at the farm to photograph Khan, there was bleating from the garage – a blackfaced Suffolk lamb that had been abandoned by its mother that morning. It was a gamble, but we took both animals into the living room. Khan automatically put a protective leg over Lucky the lamb, who within minutes had nodded off to sleep.

## 28.
## LABRADOR RETRIEVER
Spence – five years old

This is one of my favourite images. Spence is a really lazy dog – similar to my Henry. He always walks around with a gumboot, or a carrot, in his mouth. But do you think I could get him to do it for the camera?

## 29.
## IRISH SETTER
Olly – seven years old, Maddy – four years old

These two supermodels were initially nervous in front of the camera, but they relaxed knowing they had each other for support. They have become very attached to each other over the years – travelling across the world together – so they seemed to snuggle up for comfort.

## 30.
## AMERICAN PITBULL TERRIER
Jabba – eight year old

Despite the stigma attached to her breed, Jabba must be the most gentle dog I have photographed. She frequently hides behind Pooky, a Chihuahua, whenever visitors come to call, and ran terrified from the room during the photo shoot – frightened by a fly.

## 31.
## BLOODHOUND
Ben – six years old, Bella – three years old

With their trusty bloodhound noses, Ben and Bella quickly sniffed out the honey we smeared on their muzzles. The best of friends, they often give each other an affectionate lick.

## 32.
## FRENCH BULLDOG
Mr Hynds – two years old

Mr Hynds is a champion dog, so it took him only a matter of minutes to figure out how to chomp down on a pipe. His owner happily puffed away to create the smoky effect.

## 33.
## PUG
Cheeko – seven and a half years old

Cheeko was not so impressed with his moment in the spotlight. This was the last shot, as he plonked himself down on his backside as if to say "Enough!"

## 34.
## MALTESE
Phlashdance – two years old

Such a sweet, innocent-looking dog, but Phlashdance lives up to his nickname, Turbo. With tireless little dogs like him, it's best to isolate them from distractions. So Phlashdance, a showdog, was the perfect model when he finally flopped down, just him and the camera.

## 35.
## AMERICAN COCKER SPANIEL
Dominic – three years old

Dominic has so much coat, we were eternally grateful to have his owner, a dog groomer, on hand to smooth him out. He may have been only three, but he had the face of a wise old man.

## 36.
## BORDER COLLIE
Toby – two years old

Toby's family call him "The Stickman" – he is rarely without a tree branch clenched in his jaw. He agreed to play photo so long as someone threw a stick out the door into the backyard every few minutes.

## 37.
## STAFFORDSHIRE BULL TERRIER CROSS
Ramone – nine years old

Totally impromptu, Ramone vaulted on to a hay bale and sat still, the wind whipping his ears. He was supposed to share the limelight with his companion, Conan, but the older dog just couldn't make the leap. (He had his moment of glory later.)

## 38.
## CHOW CHOW
Cocoa – two months old

Babysitting Cocoa was a mission: he was two months old, but a bundle of attitude. He ran himself ragged and collapsed on the floor – the perfect time to steal a photo.

## 39.
## DOGUE DE BORDEAUX
Cujo Lexx – two months old

The Dogue de Bordeaux is an intimidating breed, often employed as a guard dog. But at two months old, Cujo Lexx was just a typical, friendly puppy, staring quizzically at the big lens.

## 40.
## DALMATIAN
Monty – five weeks old

Monty was one of 11 puppies in the litter and not supposed to be the star of the show. One of his siblings was all dressed up with gingham bows in her ears, but little Monty burned around the set until he eventually dropped down on the cushioned silk, flipped over and snoozed.

## 41.
## WEIMARANER
Bruce – three months old

Bruce simply wanted to run, leap and play – he was a very easily distracted dog. Everyone else was banished from the room so we could concentrate on the business at hand.

## 42.
## RHODESIAN RIDGEBACK CROSS
Conan the Barbarian – 11 years old

There are two sides to Conan, a very sensitive but protective dog. On the left is the true, gentle Conan. The snarling stance was to protect a bone that his owner Nathalie had placed at his feet and I attempted to steal.

## 43.
## NEAPOLITAN MASTIFF
Neo – three months old

In Roman times, Neapolitan Mastiffs were fighting dogs, bred to battle lions, bears and even elephants. But Neo was far from intimidating – all legs and head – earning the nickname "spider dog".

## 44.
## GERMAN SHORTHAIRED POINTER
Blitzen – three years old, Donner – four years old

In German, Blitzen means lightning, and Donner, thunder. Whenever we bump into them at the park, Henry sits and stares in awe as this pair of pointers stir up a storm.

## 45.
## BOXER CROSS
Zenith – seven years old

Zen is a star of the international small screen, featuring in commercials and the television series, *Hercules*. A natural born actor, he will do anything for the camera, including donning a top hat.

## 46.
## BULLMASTIFF
Illbruck & Sabrina – four months old

Getting Illbruck and Sabrina to stay still for a second was like wrestling with two maniacs. They caused total chaos running through the house, the studio, the yard…

## 47.
## ROTTWEILER
Baylee – two years old

The lens was only centimetres away from Baylee, but this gentle-natured Rottweiler was not concerned in the slightest. She was content to sit and stare longingly at the treat held just above her nose.

## 48.
## PEMBROKE WELSH CORGI
Shorts and Sox – six years old

While Sox, on the right, appears to be the one most enjoying this session, it was quite the opposite. Sox had to be retrieved from under a desk before every shot, while Shorts shadowed us everywhere and was happy to lie down wherever asked.

## 49.
## WEST HIGHLAND WHITE TERRIER
Ralph – two and a half years old

You can always find Ralph burrowing in a hole or under the couch, so to make him feel at home, we made him a cavern of his own.

## 50.
## BICHON FRISE
Floyd – 13 years old

He may be 13, but Floyd looks and acts like a puppy. It was no trouble getting him to play peekaboo from inside his white box.

## 51.
## YORKSHIRE TERRIER
My Oh My – five years old

The sight of My Oh My in her glorious full-length coat, draped out across the floor, was breathtaking. She was not supposed to be the focus of our attention that day, but how could you resist her magnificence?

## 52.
## AUSTRALIAN TERRIER
Bosco – 16 months old

Another burrowing dog, Bosco was relatively happy inside the perspex box I had made for him. But a game soon developed – he would sneak out and we would have to push him back in.

## 53.
## LÖWCHEN
Lexi – eight weeks old

The only way to catch the lightning-quick Lexi on film was to hold her aloft. It was also the safest way – we were constantly afraid of standing on this little ball of fluff!

## 54.
## IRISH TERRIER
Irish – three months old

A typical terrier, Irish was a challenge to say the least. She wanted to investigate everything, including the camera. Thankfully, she loved my sister's lime green blanket and finally lay still.

## 55.
## LHASA APSO
E. Nuff – one year old

Lhasa Apsos were once bred as ornamental dogs so "Sir Nuff" sat solemnly on the pedestal. But it was totally against his character – he earned his name by continuously being told "Enough!"

## 56.
## PULI
Lenny – four years old

The only way to find Lenny's face is when his tongue hangs out, and he had no idea where to look to say "Cheese!" He is the most comical dog, bouncing about on legs like springs under his mop of corkscrew locks.

## 57.
## STANDARD POODLE
Riot – four and a half years old, Briar – six weeks old

Together, Riot and her daughter Briar, were a picture of perfection, lying on a bed of rose petals as if it was what they do every day.

## 58.
## BORZOI
Toli – six years old

Curious, but a little timid, Toli peeked out from behind the security of a curtain at the visitors who had invaded his home.

## 59.
## SALUKI
Yana – seven years old

These elegant hounds once roamed the royal palaces of Mesopotamia in 7000 B.C. The flowing cape gave Yana the mystical, regal air of her ancestors.

## 60.
## PEKINGESE
Elmo – three years old

In Chinese mythology, the Pekingese was the marriage of a butterfly and a lion. Fifteen Pekingese dogs fluttered around our feet like butterflies. Little Elmo showed all the bravery and nobility of a lion, so he sat in a bed    of grass as if he was on the    Serengeti plains.

## 61.
## PUG
Cleopatra – three months old

With the name Cleopatra, it seemed only right that this little Pug puppy should bathe in warm milk. She was understandably hesitant about being dunked in my mother's fruit salad bowl. But her bath lasted just five minutes, compared to the hour it took to set up the shot.

## 62.
## KEESHOND
Keesha – four years old

After a romp through the long grass by the river and a swim to cool off, Keesha lay down on the river bed in rapture.

## 63.
### POMERANIAN
Furby – four months old

The night before her starring role, Furby broke a leg. Fortunately, six weeks later she hadn't grown too much more and could still slip into the largest pocket we could find – the jeans were big enough to fit five people!

## 64.
### BASENJI CROSS
Ruby – six years old

Ruby is never seen out without her jewels – usually a diamante collar. It's a fashion sense she has inherited from her always-bejewelled owner.

## 65.
### BASENJI
Tali – two years old

Basenji's are the dogs of the Pharaohs, and Tali looked at home against his desert background. But he wasn't keen on being backed into a terracotta pot for too long.

## 66.
### NEWFOUNDLAND
Henry – four and a half years old

Henry loves to sit in the park for hours, transfixed by everything around him – long enough to end up beneath a pile of autumn leaves.

Henasaurus – two and a half years old

Every spring, Henry gets a clip to help him cope with the hot summers. After one haircut, I left a mane down his back and pinned on "spikes" made from his clipped fur. He shook them off three times

before realising it was easier to keep still and bear it.

Henry & Pipi – one and a half years old

This is one of my favourite images. It took three weeks for Mark Vette (Pipi's owner) to train Henry to let the Rainbow Lorikeet climb over his face.

## 67.
### GREYHOUND
Dottie – 3 years old,

Blake – 3 months old

Dottie rarely gets to relax with five little puppies under her feet, but here she was relieved to spend a quiet moment with son Blake.

## 68.
### CHINESE CRESTED
Tiger Lilley – five years old

Tiger Lilley is a mummy's girl – she can't bear to be without her owner. So when her "mum" Pat left the room for this shot, she had to yell through the walls to keep Tiger Lilley placated.

## 69.
### BEARDED COLLIE
Baillie – ten years old

Baillie is a dog I have grown up with, owned by my friend's parents. She has always seemed like a little girl with a pretty pink bow in her hair.

## 70.
### AUSTRALIAN SHEPHERD
Pippa – four years old

Pippa always has a sparkle in her multi-coloured eyes and a spring in her step. She learned to use her

owner's back as a springboard to jump and retrieve a ball.

## 71.
### IRISH WOLFHOUND
Wings & Rana – one year old

It is hard to imagine just how tall these leggy Irish Wolfhound sisters are – the box they've squeezed into is one metre by one metre. They make a daunting sight bounding down the driveway to greet company.

## 72.
### MINIATURE SCHNAUZER
Ziggy – nine years old

This cheeky Miniature Schnauzer simply wanted to bask in the sunshine on the warmed tiles. He was puzzled why he had to hold a flower between his teeth.

## 73.
### KERRY BLUE TERRIER
Oscar – six years old

Capturing the magnificent spots on Oscar's back and the proud look on his face – at the same time – could have posed a dilemma. Yet Oscar was an extremely flexible dog who comfortably swivelled his head to smile.

## 74.
### ENGLISH SPRINGER SPANIEL
Francis of Lochranzo – six weeks old

It took a while to find the right-sized suspension spring to fit Francis – and even longer to convince the truck owner what it was for!

### 75.
### SPINONE ITALIANO
Bruno – one year old

Behind the fug of cigar smoke, Bruno could be mistaken for an influential Mafia don. But Bruno hates the taste of cigars, even unlit. He was happy to chew on the cheroot – with its end taped – as long as Nathalie smoked it for him afterwards.

### 76.
### LEONBERGER
Wookie – three years old, Martha –11 months old, Oake – six and a half months old, Mimmi – eight months old, Skye – four and a half years old

It was a daunting prospect trying to capture five of these Scandinavian dogs in the same frame. But it turned out the tough job was keeping Skye (in the foreground) awake.

### 77.
### GERMAN SHEPHERD DOG
Carlos – one year old

Carlos was puppy perfection, with his doleful eyes and his head cocked, lanky legs and those German Shepherd Dog puppy ears that almost cross over each other.

### 78.
### BORDER TERRIER
Nancy – three years old

### 79.
### BEARDED COLLIE CROSS
Griff – three and a half years old

A little encouragement is needed to persuade Griff to sit with Nancy at his feet – little Nancy likes to keep Griff in line by nipping at his ankles.

### 80.
### ENGLISH SETTER
Sam – 12 years old

One of my original shots, Sam has now passed away. But I will always remember the wise Sam as his owners did – a "gentle gentleman".

### 81.
### BULL TERRIER
Gypsy – four years old

Early one evening we took Gypsy to her favourite beach, where she ran across the black sand, chasing a stick. The only problem was sheltering from the sand and sea-salt she shook everywhere.

### 82.
### BEAGLE
Jessie – two months old

This is not a position you would normally see Jessie in – she's always on the go. We had to run her off her feet before she retired to the cosy comfort of her blanket.

### 83.
### AMERICAN BULLDOG
Shadow – one year old

This sweet little bulldog appears to have two different faces – one, like her name suggests, in shadow.

### 84.
### CHINESE SHAR-PEI
Ripley – four years old

Ripley is a tomboy, who likes nothing better than to splash in mud. A flower tucked behind her ear brings out her girlish side.

### 85.
### SPOODLE
Jack – six months old

Jack, a cross between a Cocker Spaniel and a Miniature Poodle, was a little confused by where my funny squeaks were coming from. After an eye trim, he could see all that much better.

### 86.
### LABRADOODLE
Dougal – ten months old

Dougal, a Labrador Retriever-Standard Poddle cross, isn't usually allowed on the furniture. So he thought he was in heaven when he was actually encouraged to jump up on the forbidden leather armchair.

### 87.
### ENGLISH COCKER SPANIEL
Banjo – five months old

Banjo lives on a farm, hangs out with the horses and has a relaxed saunter. He didn't mind taking time out to pose for a frame or two.

### 88.
### AFGHAN HOUND
Yasmine – seven months old

If no one is paying Yasmine the attention she craves, she literally bounces off the walls. To calm her down, Nathalie crawled under a fur rug and tickled Yasmine, who lay blissfully on top of her.

### 89.
### AUSTRALIAN KELPIE
Mocha – ten years old

**90.**
## SIBERIAN HUSKY
Cino – two years old

Although Cino had only been part of Mocha's life for two years, the two are inseparable. Cino often leans on Mocha for guidance, and the older dog proudly leads the way.

**91.**
## ROUGH COLLIE
Tui – four years old, Coco – nine years old

These two Rough Collies live and play together, and it is son Tui who dotes on, and cares for, his mother, Coco.

**92.**
## BERNESE MOUNTAIN DOG
Elvis – six months old

I was horrified… after spending weeks tending my special grass, the effervescent Elvis had flattened it all in two seconds! He sat still for just four shots – three of them were duds, but this one was perfect.

**93.**
## TIBETAN SPANIEL
Miss Ellie – eight years old

Miss Ellie loves nothing more than being cradled in her owners' arms. As soon as she was placed in her hanging crib, she drifted off like a newborn baby.

**94.**
## SOFT-COATED WHEATEN TERRIER
Arthur – two years old

Arthur is our other "office" dog, belonging to my business partners. He was incredibly business-like for the photos, and looked at me suspiciously out the corner of an eye, as if questioning my work practices.

**95.**
## OLD ENGLISH SHEEPDOG
Nelson – eight months old

Lord Nelson, as he is better known, is a "leaner" who likes to affectionately push up against people. We spent more time with him in our laps than on the set. In the end, we had to shove a couch behind him for this shot so he had the security of something to lean on.

**96.**
## IRISH WATER SPANIEL
Judy – four years old

All water spaniels love water, and Judy loves the towelling down afterwards almost as much. After a good hosing, Judy snuggled into the luxurious chocolate-brown towel that matched her heavenly coat.

**97.**
## DACHSHUND
Darcy – two years old

Intimidated by the monster-sized dogs at the park, Darcy, a Miniature Short-Haired Dachshund, seeks safety between the nearest pair of human legs. For extra reassurance she sticks her front paws on your feet, digging  in her claws, just to appear that little bit taller.

**98.**
## CAVALIER KING CHARLES SPANIEL
Teddy – one year old

Teddy was one sharp little dog. He soon figured out that the quicker we took his picture, the sooner he could retreat to his customary spot onthe couch.

**99.**
## JACK RUSSELL TERRIER
Iago – nine weeks old

Iago, a recent addition to my assistant's Italian family, is as active as he is inquisitive.

**100.**
## CHIHUAHUA
Hamish – 11 months old

**101.**
## GREAT DANE
Flynn – six years old

These are the last photos of big, beautiful Flynn – playing with tiny neighbour Hamish – taken only hours before Flynn died. While we were devastated by the news of his passing, his owners were grateful that we had captured these images to always remember him by.

Closing image
## GERMAN SHEPHERD DOG
Friedel – two years old

## NEWFOUNDLAND
Henry – eight months old

This photograph was taken in 1997 in the early stages of a very special friendship. Friedel was the first dog Henry met and they bonded instantly. But Friedel was diagnosed with cancer in 2002 and died a few weeks later. We miss her dearly.

# ACKNOWLEDGEMENTS

There are so many people to thank for their help with producing this book, it is impossible to mention every individual, but I am most grateful to you all for whatever efforts you gave. Every little bit counts.

I would firstly like to thank Nathalie Giacomelli, my faithful assistant, who has given endless enthusiasm and worked with the utmost patience needed when working with animals. This project has been as much yours as it is mine.

A special thanks to my business partners David and Tanya Todd. Your encouragement and support over the years has been invaluable and has allowed me to be as creative as I can be.

Thank you to the other members of our team in New Zealand, especially Robine Harris (design and retouching) and Sandra Seton, along with Richard Horton (UK and Europe) and Eric Kuskey (USA). You have all been invaluable in your own special ways, not only with this book but with the many other projects to date and, no doubt, in the future.

Geoff Blackwell and Ruth-Anna Hobday of PQ Publishers, I can't thank you enough for the opportunity you have given me to make my dreams come true by helping me create something so close to my heart, and which I can share with people all over the world. Thank you to all the team at PQ for being so wonderful to work with, especially Lucy Richardson who has worked so hard in creating the simple, yet beautiful design.

A special thanks to my wonderful friends Rae and John Field and their beloved Newfoundland, George. Rae also made a lot of the costumes used in the images. Henry also offers enormous thanks to you both for being his surrogate parents while Mum is so often spending time with other dogs.

Many thanks to the team at Onewa Road Veterinary Clinic in Auckland for their help introducing me to so many dogs.

There are so many others to thank including Image Centre (scanning), PCL (colour processing and prints), Labtec (black and white print processing), and Apix for their fast, efficient service in delivering my film, especially on the days I had left it to the last minute.

And of course a HUGE thanks to all the dogs and their owners for their support and enthusiasm in being part of this project.

I give my final thanks to all my friends and family for their constant support and encouragement, especially my parents Bob and Barbara and my twin sister Rebecca, who never say no to being shown yet another image for their opinion. I love you all heaps and I hope I have made you proud.

*Rachael.*

ESPECIALLY FOR FRIEDEL

SCOTT & SONIA, FRIEDEL WILL BE WITH US ALWAYS

AND FOR HENRY MILLER